SOUND and SENSE

SOUND
and
SENSE

*A Handbook
on Elocution*

by

WILTON
COLE

London
George Allen & Unwin Ltd

First Impression in 1942
Second Impression 1943
Third Impression 1945
Fourth Impression 1947
Fifth Impression 1949
Sixth Impression 1951
Seventh Impression 1953
Eighth Impression 1957

PRINTED IN GREAT BRITAIN BY

BRADFORD AND DICKENS

LONDON, W.C. I

FOREWORD

DEAR WILTON COLE,

It is a far cry from my first days at the Old Vic in 1926, when, if I remember rightly, you used to send me charming little notes of encouragement, and criticizing my short-phrasing, etc., to this year of our Lord, 1941, when you invite me to send your book off with a word of God-speed.

But I feel much the same, and when reading your book am conscious of the amount of knowledge my unknown teacher had, and still has, and a very strong feeling that it would be of the greatest value to a person learning to speak English.

I am glad to know that you think quiet, reasonable recitation is coming back. The " Ponging " School had much to answer for, and to hear lovely lines *spoken* is a rare pleasure.

Good luck to your book, and good wishes to you.

Very sincerely,

EDITH EVANS

October 2nd, 1941

PREFACE

THIS little book tries to set forth, clearly and without undue elaboration, what it is hoped may be useful to the reciter, both as teacher and performer. It is not intended for the stage artist, but rather for the artist-teacher of Elocution.

I use the word " elocution " deliberately rather than such terms as verse-speaker or diseur, both of which, though held in esteem by many, seem to me to smack of preciosity. The words " reciter," " elocution " and " recitation " began to fall out of favour many years ago owing to obvious exaggerations of speech and gesture and a general note of unreality. Although isolated instances of this may still occasionally be found, such performances are now almost non-existent; indeed the tendency now is towards undercolouring, especially in the matter of inflection which, be it remembered, is an element, although a subsidiary one, of rhythm. Let us hold the balance, and keep a sense of justness and proportion. I do not feel that it is really honouring a poet to speak his words in an expressionless tone for fear lest the speaker's personality interpose itself between the poet and the audience. As a famous actress once said to me: " You see, we are the *salt!* "

WILTON COLE.

39 Clarence Gate Gardens,
   Regents Park, N.W.1.

CONTENTS

Vowels

LET us begin with a definition.

A vowel is an element of speech, having a free passage through the mouth and shaped by the varying positions of tongue and lips.

Unlike the consonant, the vowel sound is emitted without any serious interruption, though in the case of "la*me*" and "f*eel*" the tongue-blade is raised towards the hard palate and so the passage is narrowed.

Vowels are best divided into monophthongal (one-sounding), diphthongal (two-sounding) and triphthongal (three-sounding).

In producing the monophthongal sounds the articulative organs remain steady throughout, whereas in the diphthongal sounds there is a movement from one position to another, and in the triphthongal three positions altogether.

In the following table example words are given to illustrate the vowel sounds, in order to avoid the use of phonetic symbols.

(It is necessary to distinguish carefully between a vowel *sign* and a vowel *sound*.

There are only five vowel signs—A, E, I, O, U; but there are any number of vowel sounds, twenty-six covering the ground for all practical purposes. The first letter of the Alphabet, for instance, has seven different sounds, each represented by the sign A: At, All, Rather, Any, What, Among, Lady.)

Monophthongal vowels are subdivided into open (or long) and shut (or short). Open sounds are those which are normally capable of being sustained; shut sounds are those which are normally incapable of being sustained.

Let me illustrate what I mean by speaking for a moment of the treatment of speech in song.

The singer is at the mercy of the composer in this matter. No doubt a good composer will so fit notes and words that each vowel sound will have its true value. But supposing a second-rate composer should set the word " lip " to a sustained note, what must the unfortunate singer do? Must he alter the word to " leap " ? No, the singer most certainly must not alter the character of the vowel sound, but must sustain the shut character of the sound against its normal nature, keeping the tongue in its slightly relaxed condition as against the more tense condition required for " leap."

I hope this will make clear the essential difference between open and shut vowel sounds.

MONOPHTHONGAL VOWEL SOUNDS

Open	*Shut*
Calm	Cat
Pool	Pull
Feel	Fill
Caught	Cot
Hurt	{ Hut
	{ Awake
	Wet

Diphthongal vowel sounds

Four principal diphthongs

Life = Calm + Fill
Loud = Calm + Pull
Coil = Caught + Fill
Mute = Fill + Pool

Some explanation is needed here about the analysis of " Life " and " Loud." Fifty years ago the analysis usually given of " Life " was a broad " ah " followed by a broad " ee." Then the " ee " element was felt to be wrong, and the sound as in " fill " was substituted. Further, it was felt that the " ah " of the first element was too broad, and—as so often happens in violent reactions—the pendulum swung back too much in the other direction, and the sound as in " up " was substituted, and this sound is widely taught and accepted to-day. But this is just as much too narrow a sound as the uncompromising " ah " was too broad ; moreover, a true diphthong should consist of one open and one shut element, so that the voice can rest slightly longer on one than the other. Therefore, the true analysis of the diphthong " life " should be *a light form* of the " ah " as in " calm " (something like the vowel in the French " place "), but definitely an open sound, followed by the shut i as in " fill." The same remarks apply to the first element in " Loud."

And now we come to still more controversial ground, namely, the vowel sounds in " ale " and " mole." There has always been some dispute concerning these two sounds, some holding that they are monophthongal and others diphthongal, while a third school will tell you that they are sometimes one and sometimes another according to the consonant that follows.

I think the difficulty arises from the fact that *as diphthongs* they are peculiarly English. Setting aside other European countries, if we listen to a Scotsman (one, of course, who has not become anglicized in his speech), we shall find that he will pronounce these sounds as monophthongs. It is only as we pass down into England, and more particularly Southern England, that the diphthongal quality becomes apparent.

Now, rightly or wrongly, Southern English has come to be regarded as Standard English, and therefore, so long as this is so, we must consider these two vowels as diphthongs. But there is little doubt that they are not so definitely diphthongal as the four sounds classified above as " Four Principal Diphthongs," and so they are here given the name, coined for them, I think, by Prof. Ellis, " Vanish diphthongs "—a term suggesting that the diphthongal element is very slight and very quickly disappears.

A further point which indicates that they are not true and full diphthongs appears in their analysis. Answers given by candidates in examinations often are that "*A*le " is made up of Ay + i, and " M*o*le " of oh + oo. But how, in the names of all the gods at once, can a sound consist of itself *plus* something else?

The true analysis of " *A*le " is W*e*t + F*i*ll—two shut vowels, thus indicating that " *A*le " is not a full diphthong.

" Mole " is more difficult, in fact impossible, exactly to analyse. The first element consists of a sound which is never heard by itself in English; it is almost the Italian monophthongal Ō, and this passes quickly into " Pull."

There is yet another class of diphthongs to be considered which are known as Murmur Diphthongs, a term again borrowed from Prof. Ellis.

There are four of these :—

Poor—Peer—Pair—Pore.

When the consonant R follows certain vowel sounds it has a double function to perform; it helps to form the diphthong, and then has its own consonantal value. First, it throws back a vague, indeterminate sound which is called the " murmur," and then, if conditions permit, there follows the trill. These conditions will be fully discussed when the time comes for dealing with consonants.

Again, these murmur sounds are peculiar to English. Like the vanish diphthongs they are not heard in Scotland. A true Scot in pronouncing the word " poor " will use a monophthong followed immediately by the trilled R.

Poor : when the consonant R follows the extreme lip vowel ōō the murmur sound is heard between ōō and the consonantal value of R.

Peer : the same effect occurs when R follows the extreme tongue vowel ēē, i.e. the vowel in which the blade of the tongue is in its highest position.

Pair :
Pore : } the same effect is also heard here.

[N.B. When the consonant R follows either of the two vanish diphthongs, these lose their original diphthongal quality and become monophthongs (as heard in Scottish or Italian), but the whole word is now diphthongal in virtue of the murmur thrown back from the R.]

At one time I had a good deal to do with teaching singers their speech. They would bring me songs in various languages, and I invariably found that Scottish singers would pronounce Italian far more easily than would English singers, owing to the absence equally in Italian and Scots of vanish diphthongs and murmur diphthongs and triphthongs.

Murmur Triphthongs

This brings us to the Murmur Triphthongs. There is no difficulty about these. They occur when the consonant R follows any of the four principal diphthongs. In these cases, unlike the vanish diphthongs, the principal diphthongs retain their diphthongal value, and the words are therefore triphthongal by virtue of the murmur sound thrown back from the R.

The following are examples of the triphthongal sounds : —

> Fire.
> Flower.
> Coir.
> Pure.

I would urge that these lovely sounds be given always their due value, which is such an enrichment of the

English language, and not distorted as is so often the case. For example, instead of the beautiful triphthongal effect of Fire and Flower one so frequently hears, even from educated and cultured people—" Make up the fah "; " What beautiful flahs ! "

A simple use of mnemonics is often helpful to a student. Here are a few suggestions. To memorize the open monophthongal vowel sounds :—

" Tall palms curl cool leaves."

To memorize the shut monophthongal vowel sounds :—

" Could not a just man get it? "

To memorize the principal and vanish diphthongal vowel sounds combined :—

" My house joins new roadway."

To memorize the four murmur diphthongal vowel sounds :—

" Four poor deer stare."

I have not been able to invent a sentence combining the four murmur triphthongs owing to the fact that, so far as I know, " Coir " is the only word, apart from proper names, containing that particular vowel sound.

Now I want to suggest two vowel exercises. The first is to sound all the vowel sounds which are formed principally with the lips, which I will call the " lip sequence."

Here is the mnemonic sentence for this sequence :—

" Pa shot Claud's old cuckoo."

Certain conditions must be carefully observed if this exercise is to be of real use. First, the jaw ; this must be open about the width of the thumb joint ; it must also be quite free, no hint of rigidity, and, thirdly, it must be steady, that is, it must remain open the width of the thumb joint throughout the exercise, and the only visible movement must come from the lips. Probably there will be a slight motion of the back of the tongue, especially during the last three sounds, but that need not concern us, so long as we are careful to keep the tip of the tongue in light contact with the upper part of the lower teeth. There will be found a natural tendency to draw the tongue away from the teeth for the last three sounds, and there is no harm in this, but it is advisable to insist on the contact throughout with beginners until the tongue is reasonably disciplined. The lips in this exercise should move independently of the tongue and teeth.

The second exercise is to sound all the vowel sounds which are formed principally with the tongue, which I will call the " tongue sequence."

Here is the mnemonic sentence for this sequence :—

" Ma loves her cats when they will sleep."

You will notice that both these sequences begin with the vowel sound " AH." This is a central starting-off place, the tongue sequence moving, as it were, in one direction, while the lip sequence moves in the other. In this tongue sequence similar conditions apply. The jaw must remain open, free and steady, exactly as in the lip sequence, and the tongue must keep in light contact with the upper part of the lower teeth throughout, while the blade of the tongue does the work. This, again, must move quite independently of lips and teeth. The contact of the tongue-tip and the teeth is even more important than in the lip sequence. Any withdrawing of the tongue-tip tends to make for backward and throaty production. If candidates at examinations are asked where the tip of the tongue should be in vowel formation, ninety per cent will reply " Behind the teeth." This is not enough. The word " contact " or " touching " must be brought in. " Behind the teeth " would be a perfectly correct description if the tongue were half-way down the throat. These two exercises should be very carefully practised, as the correct and easy performance of them is the foundation of all good speech.

Consonants

FIRST, a definition :

A consonant is an element of speech formed by the contact, or approximation, of two articulative organs, resulting in more or less interruption of the sound, sometimes to complete extinction.

It is important to distinguish between the " name " and the " power " of a consonant. Take the last letter of the alphabet—Z. We call it Zed : that is its name. But its " power " is the effect it has in a word, e.g. Zeal. We do not say " Zedeal " but zeal, the " power " consisting in the buzzing sound which results from the articulative organs being in a certain relation to each other. Now compare the power of Z with that of S. You will find that there is a vocal quality in Z which is absent from S ; it is possible to sing up and down the scale on the power of Z, while only unvocalized breath can be obtained from the power of S. Z is, therefore, termed a vocal or voiced consonant, while S is called aspirate or unvoiced. Further, let us compare Z with B. The power of B in current speech is almost negligible, but properly there is a slight vocal moment *before* what is called the explosion or parting of the lips. It is, therefore, like Z, a vocal consonant; but unlike Z it is impossible to sustain it. The full description of Z is " a sustained vocal consonant " while B is an explosive vocal consonant.

Applying these rules, we arrive at the following classification :—

Sustained vocal		*Sustained aspirate*	
(voiced)		(unvoiced)	
Z	(Zeal)	S	(Seal)
V	(Vane)	F	(Fane)
ZH	(Azure)	SH	(Assure)
DH	(Then)	TH	(Thin)
W	(Witch)	WH	(Which)
L			
M			
N			
R			
Y			
NG			

The last six vocal consonants have no corresponding aspirates. H is not strictly a consonant at all, seeing that there is no contact or even approximation of any two articulative organs. But it is customary to include it in a list of consonantal sounds, and therefore it must be regarded here as a sustained aspirate consonant.

The Greeks dealt with it much more satisfactorily, calling it a " breathing," and giving it a sign which was placed above the first letter of all words beginning with a vowel (and sometimes with R, if the word began with RH) ' indicating a rough breathing where the effect of H is intended, and ' indicating a smooth breathing where there is no sound of H.

Explosive vocal	*Explosive aspirate*
B (Bat)	P (Pat)
D (Dent)	T (Tent)
G (Gale)	K (Kale)

The explosive aspirate consonants are instances of those where, according to our definition, the contact results in complete extinction of all sound.

S, Z, SH, ZH, W, WH and Y are instances of approximation rather than full contact of the articulative organs.

It is usual, further, to classify consonants according to the articulative organs employed.

LABIALS

P, B, M.   (Bi-labials), full contact of both lips.
W, WH.   (Approximation only.)

LABIO-DENTAL

F, V.

LINGUA-DENTAL

TH, DH, S, Z.

Lingua-palatal

L, N, T, D, R, SH, ZH, Y.

Lingua-guttural

G, K, NG.

[This is a traditional but unsatisfactory term. These consonants are really formed by the contact of the back of the tongue with the soft palate.]

H in this classification is regarded as an Oral (or mouth) consonant.

A word on Y. This is formed by an approximation of the blade of the tongue to the back of the hard palate, and should be brought about without any jerking action of the jaw, but entirely by the action of the tongue. It is very similar to the formation of the vowel i (it), though to form the initial consonant Y more muscular action of the tongue is needed than for the vowel i (it). Say the word " Yet "; then substitute the shut vowel i for Y and the result is very similar. Now take the word " Yield " and substitute i for Y and the result is very different. It is only by that greater muscular tongue action that the word " Yield " can be properly shaped.

Compare with this the initial consonant W. It is not unlike the shut vowel sound o͝o (pull). Say the word " wet "; then substitute the vowel o͞o for W and the result is very similar. But if you take the word " Woo " and substitute oo for W, the result is very different. It is only by that greater muscular action of the lips that the word " Woo " can be properly shaped. And this greater muscular action of tongue and lips respectively should always be present in pronouncing words beginning with Y or W.

A good exercise is to make out a list of words beginning with Y, e.g. Yet, Yell, Yacht, etc., preceding each word by AH—i (it), being careful that no movement of the jaw takes place in forming Y or in the approach to it.

In the same way, making a list of words beginning with W, e.g. Wit, Well, Watch, etc., precede them by AH—ŎŌ, taking care again that there is no jaw movement in the formation of the W or in the approach to it.

There are still three minor classifications of consonants to be noticed.

Liquids. This is a term applied to those consonants which are smooth-flowing and musical, and, therefore, in their quality the most nearly allied to vowels. They generally include L, M, N and R.

Sibilants. (Hissing consonants) S, Z, SH, ZH.

Nasals. M, N, NG.

So then all consonants have at least two classifications, some three, and just a few have four. M, for example, has four classifications. It can be regarded as sustained vocal, or labial, or liquid or nasal.

There remain to be considered the Compound Consonants, i.e. those which are composed of two simple consonants from the classifications already given.

Compound Consonants

J is composed of D + ZH—Jam, Jest, Joy.

(ZH is equivalent to the French J.)

Another alphabetical sign which has the same composition as J is the soft G—Gem, Ginger.

Notice that both the elements forming J or soft G are vocal, D being explosive vocal and ZH sustained vocal.

Now, there is another compound consonant which is composed of the corresponding aspirate consonants, i.e. T and SH. This combination of sounds is commonly written CH, e.g. Chair, Choice, Chip, Church.

X is composed of (a) K + S, Excuse, Expense (both elements being aspirate).

„ „   „   „ (b) G + Z, Exist, Exult (both elements being vocal).

Q is always accompanied by u, and Qu is compounded of K + W, e.g. Queen, Quite, Quantity.

EXCEPTIONS

X = Z. When X is pronounced Z it is, of course, no longer a compound, e.g. Xylophone, Xenophon, Anxiety.

X = SH. e.g. Anxious.

Qu = K. e.g. Quay, Quoit.

CH = K. e.g. Chorister, Christian, Architect.

Two consonants which frequently cause trouble are R and S.

Let us consider R. It is a sustained vocal and also a lingua-palatal. The tongue-tip should be approximated with (not touching) the palatal ridge, the force of the breath causing the tip to vibrate, resulting in a trill. The so-called " smooth " R is not really a consonant at all, and the term is better not used. In the word " pert " for instance, the function of the letter R is to help form the vowel sound " er " ; if omitted, the word becomes " pet." The English, as a race, do not give due value to this very virile and expressive letter. But most of the old actors knew the value of it. I have a copy of *Macbeth* which I used when studying with Geneviève Ward, in which nearly all the Rs are underlined, because, at that time, I did not properly sound the letter. There are degrees of trill; it need not be trilled violently, but very often the trilling of R is actually part of its meaning, e.g. Run, Rush, Riot, Ruin.

There should always be some degree of trill if the R is followed, either in the same word or the next, by :

(1) A vowel, e.g. arose, for us.

(2) H, e.g. for him, forehead.

In some cases it should be trilled before Y, e.g. for you ; even occasionally before G, e.g. forgive, forget. It should also be trilled at the end of a phrase or sentence, e.g. for ever and ever.

Philip. Peace, Lady Constance, peace !

Constance. War ! War ! No peace ! Peace is to me a War !

If the word be pronounced " Waw " much of the emotional value of the word is lost. The ear must be the ultimate arbiter in this matter, but to be a reliable arbiter it needs to be trained. Anyway, let us see to it that the vital and virile quality of this letter is restored.

But there are many people who find it difficult to trill
R. Let them try this exercise : —

Alternate R with D (or other palatals) in conjunction
with shut vowels, e.g. oddi—orri. Concentrate mentally
on this before saying it, and then, as it were, jump on it.
It is the quick alternation of D and R that helps to
induce R.

ŏŏddi-ŏŏrri : oddi-orri : addi-arri : eddi-erri : iddi-
irri.

Inability to form a perfect S is even more widespread
than is the case with R, and is sometimes to be found in
high places on the stage. In certain cases this may be
due to malformation of the teeth when it is rather a
matter for the dentist than the teacher. Otherwise, it is
usually due to some weakness or careless use of the
tongue, especially of the tongue-tip.

To form S the tip of the tongue should be approximated (i.e. not quite a full contact) to the point where
the upper teeth pass into the gums. The sides of the
tongue meanwhile are raised so as to be in contact with
the upper teeth, the blade of the tongue is grooved, and
the teeth are closed. The air now has to pass along the
grooved channel of the tongue and force its way between
the tongue-tip and the point where gums and teeth
merge, and finally between the closed teeth. It is this
close concentration of the air which produces the hiss.
Some people find it easier to approximate the tongue-tip
to the *lower* teeth ; if the result is satisfactory there is no
reason why this should not be done.

A good exercise to improve a weak S is as follows : —

Make out a list of words beginning with S, and precede them with a palatal, preferably T. This kills two birds with one stone. First, it exercises the tongue-tip in form= ing T, and secondly, it keeps the tip away from the danger-point where it slips between the teeth and turns S into TH.

T-sow, T-say, T-sigh.

Then make out a further list of words beginning with S, in which the second letter is a palatal, e.g. snake, slave, star, and again precede by T. In this case the tongue- tip is still further protected from the danger-point by the palatal on either side of it.

T-snake, T-slave, T-star.

Another useful exercise is to make out a list of words beginning with EE, e.g. Ease, Each, Equal, Evil, etc., taking care to press the tongue-tip strongly against the lower teeth in sounding EE. This will strengthen the muscle at the tongue-tip.

Yet another suggestion is to take words ending in TH, being careful to place the tongue-tip well between the teeth, dwelling on the sound, and then sharply to with- draw the tongue while adding the plural S, e.g. Breath-s, Heath-s.

A common fault with English, though not Scottish, speakers is the practice of bridging hiatuses. This must be carefully watched and guarded against. " The idea of it " actually contains three hiatuses, but the only one likely to prove dangerous is that between the " a " of idea and the next word " of." A hiatus—or gap—occurs in speech wherever two vowel sounds come together in successive syllables, either in one word or two adjoining words. The word " hiatus " itself shows an example between the first two syllables. " I saw a ship " not infrequently becomes " I saw-r-a ship." I remember listening to a sermon in which the preacher repeatedly spoke of " the law-r-of God." If the fault is a besetting one, it is well, in speaking such a phrase as " the law of God," to pause slightly on " law " and realize that the tongue-tip is touching the lower teeth before passing on to the next word.

Another common fault occurs in the treatment of what are known as reduplicated and allied consonants. These are found when the same or closely related consonants come together in successive syllables, either in one word or in two adjoining words. " Wholly " and " Unknown " are examples of reduplicated consonants within the same word, while " Hot tea " and " Sit down " are examples respectively of reduplicated and allied consonants in succeeding words.

The proper treatment of such words is that there shall be only one contact of the articulative organs in shaping the reduplicated or allied letters, but this one contact must have both an " approach " and a " quit." It must be approached mentally—as belonging to the first word or syllable, and quitted—mentally—as belonging to the second word or syllable.

Ho-tea: this is wrong; true, there is only one contact, but it has not been approached as belonging to the first syllable.

Hot-ea: again wrong; one contact, but this time not quitted as belonging to the second word.

Hot^vtea: the contact between the two consonants is often broken. This is fussy, and quite unnecessary except for very special effects.

Hot-er tea: this is an attempt to be unusually distinct by violently kicking off the final consonant and adding a vocal sound. This is objectionable.

[Words such as latter, happy, muddle, are not examples of reduplicated consonants, as in these cases the doubled letter is, phonetically, only one.]

Although Scottish speakers rarely or never bridge a hiatus, they have another fault to which their English cousins are not so prone. They incline to tack a consonant at the end of a word on to a vowel at the beginning of the next word, e.g. " get up " becomes " getup." The only way to deal with this is to make a very clear mental picture of the *second* word and concentrate on that.

Breathing

I AM not going to spend time in explaining the anatomy of the thorax or the larynx; this can be learnt equally well from any simple text-book on the subject, e.g. Furneaux' *Human Physiology*. But I want you to remember this little fact—that all muscle has a point of origin (where it comes from) and a point of insertion (where it goes to). This will be referred to later.

During reposeful breathing or while asleep the air should be inhaled through the nose, where it is filtered, warmed and moistened. For the purposes of public speech of any kind it is necessary frankly to breathe through the mouth. The reason for this is that, whereas in reposeful breathing the air enters slowly and escapes more quickly, in any public work it is necessary to inhale quickly and let it out slowly. In order to inhale quickly and noiselessly the mouth passage must be used, as the nasal passages are not big enough for the purpose. Further, it does not mean that by inhaling through the mouth the air is not filtered; there is a second filter composed of tiny hairs lining the trachea, which are called " cilia " (eye-lashes).

A very common and tiresome fault with many students is noisy inhalation. This can easily be cured if the student will follow these very simple directions. I find sometimes that a student will take pains over a difficult exercise that they will not exert over a more simple one, thereby acting like Naaman the Syrian who, on being told to wash in the river Jordan to recover himself of his leprosy, went off in a huff. " My father, if the prophet had bid thee do some great thing, wouldest thou not have done it? How much rather then, when he saith to thee, wash, and be clean? " 2 Kings v. 13.

First, see that the mouth is sufficiently open, as in the case of the vowel sequences; secondly, be careful that the tongue does not build up at the back; thirdly, be sure that the soft palate is raised—in fact, keep the passageway unobstructed. But there is something more.

There must be no thought of having to take in breath—this is fatal; the intention must be to expand the thorax. If there is expansion of the thorax and the passage is open, the air will enter automatically and noiselessly; but if there is any concentration of thought upon the breath, at once there will be a gasping noise.

Now, on taking a breath reposefully, the diaphragm contracts slightly, thus giving slight vertical expansion; then the diaphragm relaxes and the central tendon returns to its original position. But if we are going to speak in public, then, first of all, we must inhale more deeply, and have a greater reserve of breath. How shall we achieve this? It has been argued that, since the natural breathing of repose is merely a contraction of the diaphragm resulting in a slight descent of its central tendon, we should therefore enlarge upon that and see how deep a vertical expansion we can get. If the transverse abdominal muscle is entirely relaxed, giving no support to the tendon of the diaphragm, it is possible to get a vertical expansion of $3\frac{1}{2}$ inches. This is the basis of what is known as " abdominal breathing." But it means that the important abdominal organs—stomach and liver—are pushed out of place to an undue degree, causing a considerable protrusion of the abdominal wall, which is unsightly and physically unhealthy, while the transverse abdominal muscle is left in a relaxed condition and unready to do its essential work of controlling the outgoing air, with the result that the tone is breathy and unsteady. Therefore, avoid abdominal breathing.

If, on the other hand, the transverse abdominal muscle

is contracted and the lower abdominal wall is, as a result, retracted (drawn in), the stomach and the liver will be pressed against the under side of the diaphragm so firmly that when a deep inhalation is taken and the diaphragm is contracted, the central tendon descends about half an inch only, thus giving very slight vertical expansion, and the rest of the contracting movement of the diaphragm will be in conjunction with the ribs and will result in considerable lateral expansion, but tending to an unduly high rather than central action. There is probably more control here than in abdominal breathing, but the tone is inclined to be of a hard and unsympathetic and unyielding quality. Therefore, avoid upper chest breathing.

2
Upper chest
Breathing

A further exaggerated form of upper chest breathing is what is known as clavicular breathing, in which, in addition to the " upper chest " action, there is an attempt to move the almost fixed first and second ribs, combined with a raising of the shoulders and a straining of the muscles of the neck. Therefore, avoid clavicular breathing.

3
Clavicular
Breathing

And so we come by this roundabout path to what is commonly known as " intercostal diaphragmatic " breathing, but which is better termed " Central " or " whole-chest " breathing. To speak of any form of breathing as " diaphragmatic " is not distinctive, since whatever form of breathing is adopted there must be diaphragmatic action.

4
Intercostal
Diaphramatic

It is important to ensure that the stance is good if the breathing is to be satisfactory.

For exercise purposes take a firm grasp of the ground

with your feet, heels together, with the toes pointing at five minutes to one. (While performing, allow one foot to be slightly in advance.)

Knees well braced, though not rigid. This has an effect on the upper part of the body and prevents hollow chest.

The lower abdominal wall must be held in a state of tonicity (tonic) i.e. neither contracted nor relaxed— straight, braced. This is important, as it affects the action of the diaphragm.

Shoulders well back without being too military. There is generally half an inch that we are not using, even though we may be holding ourselves reasonably well for ordinary purposes.

Head erect, the chin being neither held too high nor crushed into the neck. As G.K.C. says somewhere, " A man should have his head in the air, but not his nose in the air."

The whole body poised as if ready for flight.

It is convenient to tabulate the points of inhalation.

INHALATION

1. The lower abdominal wall must be held in a state of tonicity. This gives sufficient support to the abdominal organs to prevent too great a descent of the central tendon, as in abdominal breathing, but not so much as to prevent a reasonable descent, as in upper chest and clavicular breathing.

2. The diaphragm contracts and the central tendon

sinks $1\frac{1}{2}$ inches, *giving vertical expansion.* (As against $3\frac{1}{2}$ inches in abdominal breathing and half an inch in upper chest breathing. This has been tested by X-ray experiment.)

3. The external intercostal muscles contract, raising the ribs upwards and outwards, and at the same time drawing up the sides of the diaphragm which are attached to the six lowest rib-cartilages, thus *giving lateral expansion.* (Notice the double action of the diaphragm.)

4. The end of the sternum is pushed slightly forwards by the combined action of the diaphragm and ribs, *giving anterior expansion.*

5. The vertebral column is pushed slightly backwards by the action of the levatores costarum, which are in series with the intercostals, *giving posterior expansion.* There is thus a *proportionate* expansion in all directions.

6. The upper chest should be well carried throughout, and be regarded as a windbox, in contra-distinction to the lower part which is the bellows.

EXHALATION

It is not possible, I think, to tabulate exhalation in the same way. Remember that during inhalation the transverse abdominal muscle was in a state of tonicity. At the moment of exhalation it changes to a state of contraction. This should be a gradual process, a slow drawing in of the abdominal wall. Now call to mind what was said about all muscle having a point of origin and a point of insertion. The transverse abdominal muscle has its origin from the six lowest rib-cartilages; the diaphragm has its origin from the ensiform cartilage at the end of the sternum, in front; from the lumbar vertebrae, at the back; and *at the sides, from the six lowest rib-cartilages*. You see, the sides of the diaphragm and the transverse abdominal muscle have the same origin, and these two sets of muscles interdigitate, i.e. they interlace.

Now, when the transverse abdominal muscle is contracted these interdigitated muscles lock and the transverse abdominal muscle being voluntary (i.e. directly under control of the will) is thereby enabled to hold the diaphragm in check, releasing it gradually and allowing it to return to its arched condition of repose under perfect discipline. This is the action which is commonly known as the " abdominal press," and it controls that part of the diaphragm only which has sunk during inhalation, i.e. the central tendon.

While this is taking place the ribs must be held extended by the continued contraction of the external intercostal muscles. When the " abdominal press " has finished its work, then—*and not till then*—the external intercostal muscles begin to relax, allowing the ribs *and the sides of the diaphragm attached to them* to return to their condition of repose. At the same time the internal intercostal muscles contract and, acting antagonistically, prevent the external intercostal muscles from relaxing too quickly. Just as the abdominal muscle puts a check on the diaphragm, so the internal intercostal muscles put a check on the external intercostal muscles.

The more control that the speaker has over his exhalation the less will it be necessary for him to relax the intercostal muscles and lower the ribs.

Resonance

ALL hollow chambers above the larynx act as resonators.

Let us work upwards.

The Ventricle of Morgagni and the Cartilages of Wrisberg and Santorini are unimportant and need not detain us. The first hollow chamber of value is the pharynx, which is technically divided into the upper- or naso-pharynx, extending from the back of the nose to the back of the mouth; and the lower pharynx, extending from the back of the mouth down to the top of the larynx.

Working upwards we reach the mouth. This is the most important of the resonators for various reasons :—

(a) It is the largest.

(b) All sounds are shaped in it (even the nasal consonants).

(c) It is variable in shape, owing to the movements of tongue and lips.

(d) It is variable in substance : the hard palate making for brilliance of tone, and the soft palate combining with the lower pharynx to produce tone-colour.

Still proceeding upwards we arrive at the upper- or naso-pharynx, which co-operates with the nose both for direct and indirect nasal resonance. Direct nasal resonance is obtained through the consonants M, N and NG. In the formation of these the exit through the mouth is entirely blocked, in the case of M by the lips, in the case of N by the tongue, and in the case of NG by a combination of the soft palate with the back of the tongue.

Indirect nasal resonance is obtained from all other voiced alphabetical sounds. The tone is directed against the hard palate, and the nasal resonance is added to the mouth resonance indirectly owing to the hollow chamber of the nose immediately above.

There remain the cells and sinuses in the skull.

1. Maxillary Sinuses, one under each cheekbone.
2. Frontal Sinuses, one over each eye.
3. Ethmoid cells, behind the frontals.
4. Sphenoid Sinus—a largish cavity behind the ethmoid cells, between the back of the nose and the brain. This really consists of two cavities divided by a thin bone, each cavity corresponding to one nostril. If one should push a probe up the nostril far enough it would enter the Sphenoid Sinus. All these cells and sinuses are connected with the nose by tiny little passageways, and so indirectly with the outer air.

It is a debated point whether the thorax is to be accounted a resonator or not. I think we may say that it should not be regarded as a direct resonator like those hollow chambers above the larynx, but that it lends a sympathetic vibration to the lower notes of the voice.

FIVE QUALITIES OF THE SPEAKING VOICE

These can be summed up in the following words all beginning with F.

FIRM — FREE — FULL — FORWARD — FLOW-ING.

It will be found that every one has a natural tendency in their speech towards either firmness or freedom. Both these qualities are necessary to a good speaking voice. If the natural bent is towards firmness, and if this is not balanced by freedom, then the firm tone will become hard and even, possibly, harsh.

A good exercise for developing freedom of tone is humming, being careful that the hum is really in the front of the mouth, as it is possible to produce a kind of humming at the back of the throat. This forward hum can be tested by plucking the lips with the finger; if the hum is on the lips a bubbling sound will be produced, whereas if the hum is too far back the " bubbling " sound will be absent.

Then make out a list of words beginning with M; speak the words, dwelling slightly on the M while you note the sensation of freedom; then pass on to the rest of the word, being very careful to keep the same sensation of freedom throughout the word, e.g. M-ole, M-ist, M-oon, etc.

Deal in the same way with words beginning with H. H is a mere passage of breath through the mouth, free from all constriction. Note the absence of all constriction while producing H, and be very careful to retain the same feeling in passing to the rest of the word, e.g. H-one, H-ouse, H-oist.

Now let us take the converse case of someone whose natural tendency is towards freedom, but where this admirable quality is not balanced by firmness. Then the freedom degenerates into flabbiness, and the speech lacks grip and " bite."

In order to "firm up" the speech, practise on explosive consonants in conjunction with shut vowels, e.g. o͝ot, ot, ut, at, et, it; o͝ob, ob, ub, ab, eb, ib, etc.

The next quality of a good speaking voice is "full." This means bringing all the resonators into effective play.

In order to get mouth resonance combined with indirect nasal resonance a good exercise is to practise the two vowel sequences as given on pages 7 and 8 observing the conditions which are there set out. It is also useful to precede the vowel sounds with various consonantal sounds, bearing in mind that so far as is possible the jaw must remain steady, and open about the width of the thumb joint.

There are eight consonantal sounds to form which it is necessary to close, or nearly to close, the jaw, viz. S, Z, SH, ZH, F, V, TH, DH.[1]

An exercise to develop direct nasal resonance is to sound the six fundamental inflections successively on M, N and NG. This will bring into play all the head sinuses and cells which are connected with the nose.[2]

But the tone cannot be properly "full" unless it is also "forward."

Here are six points which will be found useful in acquiring a forward tone :

   1. (a) Open the mouth very slowly, trying to imagine that you are doing so by raising the upper jaw ;

---

[1] The compounds J, soft G, CH and X are not included here, as the element in each of them which necessitates a closed jaw is included in the eight sounds already given.

[2] The whole question of inflection will be treated fully in the chapter dealing with Modulation.

(b) this should result in giving you an " added consciousness " of the roof of the mouth ;

(c) which makes it easier to direct the tone forward to it.

2. The tip of the tongue must be in light contact with the lower teeth for all sounds except palatals and dentals. This is most important. A forward tongue makes for a forward tone, while a backwards-drawn tongue makes for a backward tone.

3. Try to be conscious of the mask of the face.

4. Alternate the vowel sounds e (wet) and a (ale). For every vowel sound there is a point on the tongue where the tongue tenses itself in order to hold its shape against the impact of the outgoing air. The vowel sound in " wet " has its tension point almost at the tongue tip, and this helps to draw the tone forward. The vowel sound in " ale " is a diphthong, the first element of which is the sound e (wet), so that the beginning of that diphthong is also instrumental in drawing the tone forward.

5. Combine labial consonants with the vowel sounds as given in 4.

6. Think of the breath as coming up from the lungs and the tone as coming down from the head, and try to poise the tone on the breath, like a boat on water, or one of those little balls which one sees in shooting galleries at fairs supported on a jet of water. The sensation to oneself should be purely one of tone, and there should be no consciousness of breath at all.

There is still one more quality of the speaking voice which must be mentioned—flowing. A jerky utterance will destroy the beauty and rhythm of the phrase, and largely distort the expression of the words themselves.

Vowel sounds are the most potent factors making for flowing speech, the consonants tending, in greater or less degree according to the nature of the consonant, to interrupt the flow.

For this reason singers as a class are hostilely inclined towards consonants, as they interfere with the tone. I once had an elocution student who was also a singer, and I remember having the greatest difficulty in making her pronounce an initial W. " World " became " 'orld," with only the vaguest suggestion of a lip movement for the initial sound. She had been carefully drilled by her singing teacher not to use the lips in such cases as it interfered with the tone.

Now, bearing in mind this quality which is inherent in the vowels, take a phrase, or a line of verse and speak it dwelling slightly on every vowel *sound* (not on every vowel sign), not omitting the consonants but passing over them very quickly, so that the voice always seems to be resting on a vowel sound with the mouth open.

Here is a suggested passage for practice :—

" O-n ei-ther- si-de the- ri-ver-lie-
    Lo-ng fie-lds o-f bar-ley- a-nd o-f rye-."

Do not sing this, but speak it with rather marked in-flections, beginning with a distinct pause on all the vowel sounds, but gradually quickening the rate and reducing the pauses until the normal delivery has been reached.

Modulation

THIS means, literally, " change," and in Elocution comprises all the ways whereby the delivery may be varied by means of the voice. Some theorists and teachers extend the term to include pause, and even gesture, but here it is intended to cover only vocal technique.

It can be tabulated under five heads :

1. PITCH.

This refers to the height or depth of the voice. Candidates in examinations will often tell you that pitch is the " tone " of the voice, to which I reply, " Do you mean loud or soft? " After which we generally arrive at the correct answer.

The different pitches merge one into another, and there is no clearly marked line where one pitch ends and the next begins. But we may say, roughly, that there are three pitches, high, middle, and low.

There are four reasons for changing pitch during performance :

(a) Change of emotion, e.g. happiness or excitement will take a high pitch, while sorrow or solemn utterance will take a low pitch.

A medium pitch will naturally be used in unimpassioned lines, or colloquial prose.

(b) Characterization.

If one performer is playing a scene in which two or more characters are speaking, especially if the

c) Emphasis

characters are male and female, the speakers must
be differentiated in pitch. A woman will always
speak on a higher pitch than a man, whatever the
emotional expression. A boy and girl of ten will
both use a high pitch, but the same boy and girl,
arrived at the age of seventeen, will no longer use
the same pitch, as the boy's voice has now "broken,"
and his pitch will consequently be lower than that
of the girl. A very old man will probably tend
towards a high pitch,

> "   and his big manly voice,
> Turning again towards childish treble, pipes
> And whistles in its sound." [1]

(c) Change of paragraph or subject matter.

(d) In speaking a parenthesis.

A parenthesis should always be spoken on a
different pitch, more usually, though not necessarily,
on a lower pitch. When more than one parenthesis
occurs in succession it is useful to place one of them
on a higher pitch.

> " For the highway
> Is flowerless, and thin the mountain air,
> And rends the lungs that breathe it, and
>   the light

1st parenthesis.	/Spreading from hill to everlasting hill,
2nd „	/Welling across the sky as from a wound,

----

[1] *As you like it.*

3rd parenthesis.   /A heart of blood between the breasts
                        of the world,
                     Is not much nearer, no, nor half as
                        warm
                     As the kissing sun of the valleys." [1]

Here there are three successive parentheses.   It is
suggested that the first be spoken on a slightly lower
pitch than the main sentence, that the second be
spoken on a pitch slightly higher than the main
sentence, while the third and last parenthesis be
spoken on a much lower pitch, thereby making a
marked change of note on resuming the main
sentence.   *2nd Par.*

Main sentence.   1st Par.   *Main sentence.*

               3rd Par.

There should always be a slight pause both before
and after a parenthesis.   In the case of two or more
parentheses the first and last pauses should be longer
than the others.

A reason for changing pitch which is frequently
put forward is that it must be done " to avoid
monotony."   It is true that it does help to avoid
monotony, but it must not be done solely for that
reason.   There are many other ways of avoiding
monotony, and pitch should only be altered for the
four reasons given above.

---

[1] Will Shakespeare (Clemence Dane).

2. INFLECTION.

I am going to write at some length on this point because I find in the course of teaching that there is a great deal of uncertainty in regard to it, both theoretically and practically, an uncertainty which is not altogether dispelled by many of the text-books which deal with the subject.

When I was a young student of elocution I was taught almost entirely through a system of inflection, and was taught very little else; all other fundamentals of speech and voice production I had to pick up for myself subsequently. I am not advocating this system of elocutionary training, but there is this to be said for it. In these days of lectures on all possible branches of our subject, of classes dealing with every phase of the work, of intensive preparation for examinations there is danger of students becoming spoon-fed, and not really assimilating all the nourishment whereas, when one has to delve for oneself, to test, accept and reject on one's own initiative, the resultant knowledge sticks.

But to return to inflection.

The result of my rather specialized training in the subject is that I am perhaps more critical in regard to it than to other points of technique, and it seems to me that many writers are most misleading and confusing—dare I say " confused " ?—on the subject. *The Pronunciation of English* by Prof. Daniel Jones [1] is a brilliant exception,

---

[1] I am speaking here only of inflection and intonation. The question of pronunciation, as dealt with by Prof. Jones, is perhaps more debatable.

and is really wonderful in its analyses of inflection and intonation, and denotes an exceptionally keen ear to be able to describe so accurately the most delicate nuances of the vocal scale.

In the bad old days, inflection, like gesture, suffered from over-indulgence, and the voice was made to rise and fall so wildly that the passage was as uneven as Falstaff's sword after the affair at Gadshill. Sometimes an inflection would take such an upward or downward sweep that the listener would be in doubt whether the speaker had not actually altered his pitch. For, remember, pitch and inflection are intrinsically different. In a sense, of course, an inflection will slightly alter the pitch, but in the strictly technical and specialized sense pitch is the note on which a whole passage is spoken, which will only be altered for very definite reasons as given in the section on Pitch; whereas, inflection is the gentle rise and fall of the voice on the syllables of that passage *within the pitch;* so that one may use falling inflections within a high pitch and rising inflections within a low pitch without any change of pitch in either case. That bad use of inflection is, happily, a thing of the past, but as is the case with all reactions and revolutions the pendulum has tended to swing too far in the opposite direction, and there is a school of thought among us to-day which is inclined to look upon all inflection as of the devil, and to eliminate it altogether.

Of course, the degree of inflection will vary according to the character of what is being spoken. Speaking broadly, a dramatic selection will require more marked

inflections than a lyric, and the more lyrical the poem the
more modified must be the inflection, but it should never
be eliminated altogether. Directly this happens it is no
longer speech, but a sort of hybrid between speaking and
singing, and at once reality is lost, and the result is deadly
monotony. Very different from this is that disciplined
vocal modulation, of which inflection is an important
element, which can indicate subtly but surely the infinite
variations of lyrical feeling without disturbing the melodic
line.

A charge often brought against the great Sarah
Bernhardt was that in speaking verse she chanted the
words. This was not so : the sensitive ear could always
catch the fine shades which differentiate speech from intoning, though it must be borne in mind that the French
language has not the same stress-value, and consequently
not quite the same quality of inflection as the English,
and further that the famous *voix d'or*—a voice like the
glory of sun upon the sea—tended to underline the
musical value of the words, and so to approximate them
to the nature of song. The truth was well expressed by
the *Morning Post* [1] when speaking of her *L'Aiglon,* " The
words and lines drop from the lips with the clear yet ever-
changing tone of the waterfall."

I think it may be said that it requires more vocal
discipline and breath-control to treat inflection rightly in
a lyric than in a dramatic selection ; because, whereas in
dramatic work the inflection can be broad and incisive,
in a lyric the slightest vocal glide must be made signifi-

[1] *Morning Post,* June 4th, 1901.

cant, and this naturally needs the most perfect technical mastery.

I have no intention of giving a lot of complicated rules; a few general principles should be enough for the intelligent speaker. The most important thing of all is to have a keen ear, to be able to distinguish when the voice rises and when it falls. One might suppose this to be a simple matter, but it is just here that so many students find difficulty.

There are only six fundamental inflections,[1] although, of course, there are infinite degrees of these six. Here they are: Simple rising ╱ : simple falling ╲ : circumflex rising ◡ : circumflex falling ◠ : compound rising ∿ : compound falling ⌇. Let us illustrate them by this simple dialogue :—

Is it black or white?

It's blue.

Blue? (retorted question).

I think so.

Well!

And mark this. In regard to the dual and triple inflections *it is the final direction which determines its character.* This is where many students go wrong. You suggest a rising inflection, and in their wild endeavour to carry it out they slide the voice up quite a long way

[1] Although, in certain exceptional cases, four-directional inflections may be met with, these instances are so rare that it does not seem desirable to confuse the main issue by including them in the above table.

and then spoil it all by slightly turning the inflection down at the end, so that, in spite of the fact that it has a far greater proportion of ascent than descent, it has definitely the character of a falling inflection. I have sometimes found that a student who is inflection-dull can get the right effect by deliberately trying to inflect in the opposite direction. For instance, if he has difficulty in inflecting upwards, make him think downwards and he will probably give it that little extra kick upwards at the bottom of the glide which will give it the character of a circumflex rising inflection; and gradually he will come to hear and realize what is happening, and be able to distinguish the various glides of the voice. Now a falling inflection, speaking broadly, has the effect of definiteness, *completeness* affirmation, conclusion, and if the student gives the character of a falling inflection to intended rising ones the result is to introduce too many final points and destroy continuity. Suspensive clauses demand a rising intonation. Shakespeare is very fond of introducing long suspensive passages, during which the phrases pile up and up until a single line supplies the conclusive clause, and provides the opportunity for the voice to fall.

> ·" *those opposed eyes*
> Which, like the meteors of a troubled heaven,
> All of one nature, of one substance bred,
> Did lately meet in the intestine shock
> And furious close of civil butchery,
> *Shall now,* in mutual well-beseeming ranks
> *March all one way.*"
>
>   *Henry IV*, Pt. 1. Act I, Sc. 1.

D

Give this passage to a student to read at sight, and in nine cases out of ten he will bring the voice down on " butchery "; but this marks the end of the suspense and must receive a rising inflection. The italicized words show the main sentence; all the rest is suspensive and parenthetic, and the falling inflection is only introduced on the last word " way." The first four lines of Keats' *Ode on a Grecian Urn* are suspensive, an invocation leading up to the question of the fifth line—a question which takes a falling inflection and provides the conclusive clause. A striking instance is to be found in Keats' *Ode to Autumn,* where the whole of the first stanza, in spite of the full stop usually printed after " clammy cells," really forms one long suspensive clause leading up to the question " Who hath not seen thee oft amid thy store ? " It should be superfluous to say that there need be no monotony in such treatment. Although it may be necessary to employ rising inflections for a considerable passage without the variation of falling ones, the degrees of inflection are infinite, and, moreover, inflection is only one of many ways of modulating the voice.

Here it may not be out of place to note a fixed idea held by many students that a question always takes a rising inflection, whereas all phrases introduced by How, Which, Who, What, Why, etc., normally take a falling inflection, unless it is what is called a retorted question.

As it is necessary to use rising intonation for suspensive passages, so a conclusive clause requires a falling inflection. It is a good working rule to cut out all unnecessary falling inflections because, as I said above, they tend to destroy continuity. At the same time there are exceptions to this as to every other rule, and to employ a falling inflection in the middle of a phrase may be a means of making an important word stand out and become significant.

There is a curious tendency on the part of some students—I have noticed it frequently at Festivals—to end a poem with a rising inflection. This is an exceedingly dangerous practice, and although I would not go so far as to say that it should never be done, it must be done with the utmost discretion and not without a very strong reason, as the effect is one of inconclusion, something like an interrupted cadence in music—or, as I once heard it called inadvertently but I think very happily and expressively, a " disappointed " cadence. Ellen Terry, in her *Memoirs,* gives an instance which is worth underlining. It was in her younger days, and it fell to her lot to speak the last words of the play. Owing to the theatrical superstition that it is unlucky to speak the final " tag " before the first public performance, the words were never rehearsed. On the first night Ellen Terry delivered the passage with a rising inflection. There was a long pause, the curtain did not come down, and the effect of the scene was nearly ruined. She ends the story in these words : " For the credit of my intelligence I should add that the mistake was a technical one, not a stupid one. The line was a question. It *demanded* an upward inflection ; but no play can end like that."

From time to time correspondence appears in the

Church newspapers concerning the reading of the lessons and other parts of the service, and someone always writes to say that the remedy for inaudibility is to keep the voice " up " at the end of sentences. Now what does this mean? To begin with it is advisable to distinguish between audibility and distinctness. In the Book of Common Prayer the rubric preceding the reading of the lessons begins: " Then shall be read distinctly with an audible voice . . ." Audibility depends on the resonant quality of the voice acting chiefly on the vowel sounds while distinctness is a matter of exact articulation of consonants. What does this " keeping the voice ' up ' " mean? I am afraid that, in the minds of the writers, it often means an upward inflection. But the end of a sentence generally denotes some rounding off of the sense, and therefore demands a falling inflection. No, the remedy is not to alter the inflection against the natural sense, but to see to it that you observe four things:—(1) good breath control; (2) good breath pressure behind the words; (3) exact articulation of final consonants; and (4) care that the final falling inflection is gradual and not sheer.

A pupil will sometimes say to me: " I can't get that inflection; won't mine do as well? " My answer is: " Yes, so far as the interpretation is concerned your inflection is perhaps just as good as mine; but you should be *able* to take any inflection at will." So we come back to the importance of the ear. Of all the senses the most important for the elocutionist is that of hearing. But the ear must be trained before it can become reliable. Train the ear to recognize the direction of the voice-glides. Some people are quicker than others to detect these glides, but very few are so inflection-dull that they cannot improve. And you who do possess the gift of a keen ear, don't think that a knowledge of the technique of inflection doesn't matter. It matters very much—especially if you are teachers.

3. RATE.

The rate of utterance of any passage must be determined by two things :—

(a) The nature of the passage.

(b) The capabilities of the speaker.

The following lines from Tennyson's *Ulysses* obviously call for a slow rate of delivery :—

" The long day wanes; the slow moon climbs; the deep
   Moans round with many voices "—

These lines, on the other hand, from Hilaire Belloc's *Tarantella,* need a rapid delivery :—

" Do you remember an inn, Miranda?
   Do you remember an inn?
   And the tedding and the spreading of the straw for
      a bedding,
   And the fleas that tease in the high Pyrenees,
   And the wine that tasted of the tar? "

But when a rapid delivery is needed the speaker must be careful that the articulation is clean and distinct. Some people can naturally articulate more rapidly than others. It amounts to this : a passage must not be spoken at a faster rate than the speaker can clearly articulate. This may sound obvious, but no one with experience of teaching can doubt the importance of stressing it.

4. TONE AMOUNT.

There is little that need be said on this head. It includes the whole range of loud and soft tones from ff. to pp. Be chary of extremes : keep them for special effects.

5. TONE QUALITY.

I want you to notice that all these five points of modulation have opposite possibilities :

Pitch—high or low.

Inflection—rising or falling.

Rate—fast or slow.

Tone amount—loud or soft.

Tone quality—hard or soft, sympathetic or unsympathetic.

Modulation is sometimes spoken of as consisting of Pitch, Pace and Power. This has the virtue of being alliterative and therefore easily remembered, but it is not sufficiently embracing, and the word " Pace " is not quite a satisfactory substitute for " Rate," as it has a specialized technical meaning of its own, which will be dealt with later.

In tone quality may be included " Intensity." This is often confused with " Restraint " but is really quite different. Restraint demands that considerable power be held in reserve, and the audience is subconsciously aware of this, whereas in intensity all the performer's powers are brought into play, but in a highly concentrated form, compressed into a very narrow focus, like the effect of the rays of the sun through a burning glass.

The greatest exponent of both these qualities—restraint and intensity—that I have ever seen was Sarah Bernhardt, and the play, " *Pelleas et Melisande* " well illustrates them both.

I have often watched performances which have been called " restrained " when there has been precious little power to restrain; but in the scene by the well, where Melisande shows the ring to Pelleas, one saw an actress whose power seemed almost unlimited speaking the words with a quiet but pregnant significance which held the audience spellbound.

Again, in the later scene when Melisande appears at a window and lets her long hair fall over the face of Pelleas who is standing below, the passion of Pelleas was let loose, but in a concentrated whisper which swept through the theatre like a scorching flame.

Both these qualities are very rare on the stage to-day; indeed, the only living actress who seems to possess intensity to any considerable degree is Haidée Wright.*

Pause

THE use of pause occupies a very important place in the work of a public speaker, whether orator, reciter, clergyman or actor. A great deal has been written about different kinds of pause, and much subtle differentiation drawn between oratorical, rhetorical, dramatic and emotional pauses.

* Since these words were written this exquisite artist has passed away.

For all practical purposes one may classify pauses under five heads :

1. Grammatical or Sense pause.

This is indicated by punctuation. But a word of caution is necessary here. Not all writers are impeccable in their punctuation, even the best of them err sometimes; so do not trust blindly to punctuation. Be guided always by the sense; this will be treated more fully when dealing with phrasing.

Instances of wrong punctuation :
" Where, do you imagine, she would lay it ? "

GEO. MEREDITH.

" Any of which peccadilloes, if Miss Sharp discovered, she did not tell them to Lady Crawley."

THACKERAY.

2. Suspensive pause.

This is found only in verse, and is used in cases of enjambment, i.e. where the sense of one line is continued without break into another. The pause is used to indicate that the end of a line of verse has been reached, but no new breath must be taken during the pause as the sense is carried on unbroken. The pause is merely a slight dwelling on the last word or syllable.

" If one could have that little head of hers
Painted upon a background of pale gold."

A Face. R. BROWNING.

" Whether 'tis nobler in the mind to suffer
  The slings and arrows of outrageous fortune."

Hamlet.

" Then hearken how the poplar trees unfold
  Their buds— "

Song of Poplars. ALDOUS HUXLEY.

Sometimes in the later plays of Shakspere, and else-
where, a line ends with some quite unimportant word,
as " to," " and," " is," etc. In such cases the pause
should be thrown back on to the last previous word that
is able to bear it.

" These our actors,
As I foretold you, were all spirits and
Are melted into air, into thin air.

Tempest. Act IV. Sc. 1.

" Shall I abide
In this dull world, which in thy absence is
No better than a sty ? "

Antony and Cleopatra. Act IV. Sc. 13.

" in which time she purposed
By watching, weeping, tendance, kissing, to
O'ercome you with her show."

Cymbeline. Act V. Sc. 5.

" The same that oft-times hath
Charmed magic casements."

Ode to a Nightingale. KEATS.

" live hair that is
Shining and free."

The Great Lover. R. Brooke.

Occasionally one meets with examples of internal enjambment calling for an internal suspensive pause.

" Oh light our life in Babylon, but Babylon has taken
    wings,
  While we are in the calm and proud procession of
    eternal things."   *Babylon.* A. E.

Here there is a slight suspensive pause on the word " proud " as it forms an internal enjambment with the remainder of the line.

3.   Cæsural pause.

This, like the suspensive pause, is found only in verse. It is the natural break that the voice makes in the large majority of the longer lines of verse for the sake of rhythm.

It is a rhythmical pause.

The most fruitful source of cæsura is the line of five feet, whether blank or rhymed.   In this line the cæsura may be found in nine different positions, from the half of the first foot to the half of the fifth.

(a) " Sléep ⋮ that | kníts úp | the ráv | elled sléeve | of cáre
(b) " You láck | the séa | son of | áll ná | turcs ⋮ sléep." [1]

Macbeth.

The word " cæsura " means literally " cutting "; it divides the line into two balancing parts.

---

[1] Here are shown examples of the cæsura (a) at the half of the first foot, and (b) at the half of the fifth foot.

The cæsura [1] generally coincides with the sense pause, but it need not do so.

4. Metrical pause.

This pause, unlike the cæsura, is an integral part of the metrical pattern, and corresponds exactly with a rest or a tied note in music. Sometimes it will cover a whole foot, sometimes only part of one.

" Hapless | doom of | woman | ⌒ | happy | in be |
    trothing

  Beauty | passes | like a | breath and | love is | lost
    in | loathing."   *Queen Mary*. TENNYSON.

The second line is metrically complete and shows the pattern. In the first line there is a whole foot missing from the pattern, and this is the metrical pause.

5. Pause for effect.

This includes oratorical, rhetorical, dramatic, and emotional pauses. It is used to make a word stand out, or to help in building up a climax, and can be placed either before or after the word to be emphasized. It is found in both prose and verse.

" When I burned in desire to question them further they made themselves air, into which they vanished."

Macbeth.

There is a tradition that Lady Macbeth should pause before speaking the word " air," to underline the weirdness of the passage. Indeed, Ellen Terry used not only to pause, but read the whole sentence over again.

[1] A further note on the cæsura is given on page 81.

" I am hushed until our city be afire
And then I'll speak a little."

Coriolanus.

Geneviéve Ward, the greatest Volumnia of her day, used to pause after " speak," so marking the contrast between " hushed " and " speak." Indeed, the word " speak " was given a falling inflection and made the final cadence, the following words " a little " being treated as of slight importance.

These quotations illustrate the use of the " pause for effect " both before and after the vital word.

Pace

I SAID above that I deprecated the use of the word "pace" in Modulation as a synonym for "rate" because it had a specialized technical meaning, and I propose to speak of it here.

" Pace " is much the same as " timing," though it has a somewhat wider application.

It is keeping one's audience continuously interested by giving them a series of mental shocks by means of various technical devices. The audience, of course, should be totally unaware that this is being done to them, and should react quite unconsciously. These technical devices may be grouped under five heads :

1. Significance.

This is one of the blessed words of Elocution. Others are " suggestion " and " sensation."

One should determine what is the important word in a phrase and speak it significantly. By " significantly " I mean make the word " tell," make it " stand out," point it. There are various ways of doing this, by pause, stress, inflection and other vocal means.

2. The subtle use of pause.

This use of pause is something different from any of the five kinds of pause already mentioned. It is the slight dwelling on a syllable, or even on a single letter before the significant word.

> " What a piece of work is a man! . . . . . .
> . . . . . . And yet, to me, what is this
> quintessence of dust? "

> *Hamlet.*

Here, a slight prolongation of the S of " this " helps to point " quintessence of dust.'"

3. Variation of spacing.

By this is meant that in cases where several short phrases or lists of words follow each other the pause length between the phrases or words should be varied, the first and last generally being the longest, while the middle ones are shorter, thus giving a quickening-up effect.

> " You see me, lord Bassanio, where I stand
>   Such as I am : though for myself alone
>   I would not be ambitious in my wish,
>   To wish myself much better ; yet for you

> I would be trebled twenty times myself;
> A thousand times more fair, ten thousand times
>   more rich;
> That only to stand high in your account,
> I might in virtues, beauties, livings, friends,
> Exceed account."

Merchant of Venice.

Here, the words "beauties, livings," should be quickened, closed up, then a longer pause, thus making the important word "friends" stand out.

> "What men or gods are these? What maidens loth?
> What mad pursuit? What struggle to escape?
> What pipes and timbrels? What wild ecstasy?"

Ode on a Grecian Urn. KEATS.

It is suggested that there might be a quickening and closing up of the phrases in the first two lines, then a slowing down, and a longer pause before the last phrase, bringing out the long quantity of the "wild."

4. Onomatopœia.

This is the artifice of making the word sound like its meaning, and this "word-painting" is always going on to a greater or less degree. English is an extraordinarily onomatopœic language, and a good use of this technical means of vocal expression can heighten the value of a word or passage very considerably.

In order to give the fullest effect to onomatopœia, it is necessary that each letter of the word should contribute its quota; so each letter must be perfectly formed and produced. Any letter which is imperfectly produced detracts from the full value of the colour effect. Some letters, of course, will contribute more than others. In the word "scream," for instance, the last letter M will have less to say in the colour scheme than the other letters. Or in the word "smooth" it is the first letter which will contribute least. Above all, the imagination must be alive. Granted these conditions, onomatopœia is one of the most potent ways of keeping an audience interested, as all great actors know.

All the great poets realized the value of onomatopœia, with which may be combined "quantity," which is a fruitful means of achieving onomatopœia.

"Quantity" is the actual duration in time occupied in speaking a syllable. The rules for determining quantity are not so strictly formulated as in classical times, but there are certain guides which may be helpful. A syllable, for quantitative purposes, must be reckoned from one vowel sound to the next, including all intervening consonants. If a syllable so reckoned contains an open vowel sound, that syllable is, *ipso facto,* a long quantity syllable; but if the syllable so reckoned contains a shut vowel sound, it does not necessarily follow that it is a short quantity syllable, because it may be lengthened by the intervening consonants, e.g. "Cool-air" —a long quantity syllable, since the syllable contains an open vowel sound; "Shut up"—short quantity syllable, as the syllable contains a shut vowel sound, and is not appreciably lengthened by the intervening consonant T.

But " shouldst not " is a long quantity syllable, since although the syllable contains a shut vowel sound it is definitely lengthened by the consonants intervening before the next vowel sound, viz. ldstn.

And here it is necessary to correct a common delusion. Stress does not affect quantity. No amount of stress can lengthen a syllable : they are two totally different things. Stress is *degree* of effort : quantity is *extent* of effort.

5.   Antithesis.

The speaker cannot, of course, *create* antithesis if the poet has not supplied it, but when it is present a pointed treatment of it is a most helpful way of giving one's audience a mental jolt.

There are four kinds of antitheses, simple, double, triple, and implied.

Here is an example of single antithesis :—

<blockquote>
" I do believe,
Induced by potent circumstances that
You are mine *enemy,* and make my challenge
You shall not be my *judge.*"
</blockquote>

Henry VIII.

Double antithesis :—

This is the most common form of antithesis.
" Think, when *we talk* of horses that *you see* them."

Henry V.

" *Speech* is *silver :* but *silence* is *golden.*"

Triple antithesis (rare) :—

> " If *one of mean affairs*
> May *plod* it in a *week,* why may not *I*
> *Glide* thither in a *day.*"

Cymbeline.

> " Nevermore apart you found
> *Her he throned* from *him she crowned.*"

" What a pretty tale." BROWNING.

Implied antithesis :—

> " But were I Brutus
> And Brutus Antony, there were an Antony
> Would ruffle up your spirits, and put a tongue
> In every wound of Cæsar, that should move
> The *stones* of Rome to rise and mutiny.
> (Implication : let alone you men of flesh and blood.)
> You are not blocks, you are not stones, but *men.*"

Julius Caesar.

Some Hints on Pronunciation

IN England we have no authoritative body for regulating pronunciation, such as the Academy of Letters in France, or even the Théâtre Français. True, there is the B.B.C., but whatever we may think of its suitability as arbiter in such a matter, it is not yet sufficiently venerable to claim our unquestioning allegiance. Therefore we are thrown back on the dictionary; but even here there is disagreement. Some dictionaries will give alternative pronunciations, others only one. I think the nearest we can get to it is to say that pronunciation should be based on " the

general consensus of educated opinion as expressed in the
best dictionaries." If there still remains uncertainty the
teacher must assume the role of dictator and pronounce
judgment.

I remember when, in 1923, we were celebrating the
centenary of the R.A.M. that word was in everybody's
mouth. And I noticed that there were two pronunciations—centénary (with a short e) and centénary (with a
long ee), but both having the strong stress on the second
syllable, and I supposed that I was the only person in
the Academy who insisted on his students speaking of
" céntenary." Then the R.A.M. club magazine appeared
with an article by one of my fellow professors who also
had noticed this discrepancy, and in order to be on the
right side had looked up the word in the dictionary
where—to his surprise—he found it was neither one nor
t'other, but " céntenary." He told me that he had
collated seven dictionaries and that they all gave " céntenary."

I think this is an instance of pronunciation being in-
fluenced by hurry or laziness. People will not be bothered
to pronounce correctly. It is so much easier to say
" labóratory " than " láboratory," or " indispútable "
than " indísputable." But we—teachers of speech and
trainers of youth—are, or ought to be, the salt of the
earth in this respect. Further—to forestall criticism—
there is no reason why such accuracy should result in
overprecision or affectation of speech. It is a matter of
getting the articulative organs under control and then
one pronunciation is as easy as another.

Here are a few words which are constantly being mispronounced.

(The strong stresses are placed here correctly.)

Éxquisite.   Ápplicable
Déspicable.   Románce
Cóntroversy.
Consúmmate (adjective). ⎫ In all three cases the " u "
Cónsummate (verb).   ⎬ is short as in " sum."
Consummátion (noun).   ⎭
Précedent (noun).
Precédent (adjective).

" 'Twill be | recór | ded for | a pré | cedent."
                              Merchant of Venice.

" A slave, that is not twentieth part the tithe
  Of yóur | precé | dent lórd."
                              Hamlet.

Precédence.
Incómparable.

" Yet shall your ragged moor receive
  The incóm | para | ble pómp | of éve."
                The House Beautiful.   R. L. STEVENSON.

Inéxplicable.
Indíssoluble.

                         " my duties
        are with | a móst | indís | solu | ble tíe
        For ever knit."
                              Macbeth.

Círcumstance—the last syllable should be neutralized.

Another class of words in which slovenly articulation is common is that in which the word ends in " ity."

> Humility.
> Integrity.
> Unity.
> Trinity.

Here the penultimate syllable often becomes neutralized, giving a dull edge to the word and actually depriving it of some of its sense-value. And *do* let us avoid neutralizing the little word " to." I am not referring to colloquial and conversational speech but to public utterance, more especially the speaking of poetry, whether prose or verse. This is a constant fault of students, and candidates for examinations, and it is the result of *sheer laziness*. Imagine the effect on a sensitive audience if an actor were to speak the opening words of *Hamlet's* famous soliloquy : —

> " Ter be or not ter be— "

It will commonly be found that in words like " golden, garden, burden," the final N rightly tends to neutralize the e, whereas in words like " jewel, duel, cruel," it is essential that the e be given its clean, shut vowel quality as in " bell," and that the words are not pronounced " jool, crool," as is so often the case.

I remember Sir Henry Irving speaking the word " jewels " in *Becket*. Irving's speech was often criticized adversely, but he both could and, at times, did pronounce individual words more beautifully than any one I have ever heard. On this occasion his speaking of the word

" jewels " was like a connoisseur tasting a choice old
wine.

" Tho' all the loud-lunged trumpets upon earth
  Blared from the heights of all the thrones of her Kings,
  Blowing the world against me, I would stand
  Clothed with the full authority of Rome,
  Mail'd in the perfect panoply of faith,
  First of the foremost of their files, who die
  For God, to people heaven in the great day
  When God makes up His jewels."

Although I heard this nearly forty years ago it still
remains a clear and beautiful memory.

There are, too, certain words whose quantitative value
is very commonly disregarded. " Modern," for example,
becomes " mod'n," " govern " " gov'n." In these words
the first syllables show strong stress and short quantity,
while the second syllables show weak stress and long
quantity. Students generally find it difficult to convey
long quantity without at the same time giving to the
syllable an added stress-value : they *think* in terms of
stress.

Agony : ⎫ These words have a strong stress on the
Melody : ⎭ first syllable, but a definitely long quantity
value on the second syllable. The O should certainly
not be neutralized, neither should it be a shut sound as
in " hot," but should have the sound of O as in " open."
Singers are often sinners in this respect.

Conversely, unless there is some special reason to bring
it out, the conjunction "and" should always be shortened

to " 'nd." Let us have the final d—not " black 'n' white,"
but " black 'n*d* white."

Lastly, I would plead for " again " to be pronounced
as rhyming with " men " and not with " pain." Even if
poets rhyme it with " pain " and " rain " it should be
regarded as an eye-rhyme, and still be pronounced to
rhyme with " men," exactly analogous to " love " and
" grove."

Prosody

THIS subject really requires a book to itself. All I propose to do here is to put forward a few suggestions for the
scanning of verse, illustrating them with actual passages
from poems. To those who wish to go thoroughly into
the subject I would recommend *The Making of Verse*,
by Swann and Sidgwick (Sidgwick and Jackson); *The
Principles of English Prosody*, by Lascelles Abercrombie
(Secker); *The Metres of English Poetry*, by Enid Hamer
(Methuen); and, from the more historical aspect, *Manual
of English Prosody*, by George Saintsbury (Macmillan).

First, two definitions :—

Rhythm.

Rhythm is the musical flow of either prose or verse,
which is brought about, chiefly, by the alternation, not
necessarily regular, of stronger and weaker stress.

Many students if questioned on rhythm will show by
their answers that they are confusing rhythm with metre,
and if you suggest that rhythm may be found in prose,

they will reluctantly allow that rhythm may be found in good prose, but they are not enthusiastic over the idea.

But it is difficult, if not actually impossible, to get away from rhythm. It may be bad rhythm, jerky rhythm, unsuitable rhythm, what you will, but it will be rhythm of a sort. Unless each syllable has the same degree of accent and quantity some kind of rhythm will result.

Now look again at the definition. First, the word " stress." This is the force or " ictus " of the voice on a given syllable, and is never found pure, but is always accompanied by inflection, the combination of the two—stress plus inflection—making accent. Inflection is, therefore, an element in rhythm, although a subsidiary one. Another secondary but not unimportant element of rhythm, which is not included in the definition, is quantity. Therefore the word " chiefly " is inserted to indicate that, although the most important element is stress, there are other elements.

Further, it must be realized that there is a certain stress on every syllable of a word, though they differ in degree. Therefore it is not strictly correct to speak of absence of stress, and so the definition speaks of stronger and weaker stress.

Finally, the alternation of stronger and weaker stress is not regular, even in verse. It is only in the under-lying pattern that the strong stresses recur regularly. And this brings us to the second definition.

Metre.

Metre is rhythm which is heard through all its varia-tions with reference to a persistent and unaltering pattern. (This definition is taken from Lascelles Abercrombie's *Principles of English Prosody*.)

Metre is found only in Verse.

The word " verse " has two legitimate uses :—

(1) It may be used to denote metrical composition generally.

(2) It may be applied to a single line of metrical composition.

But it must not be confused with " stanza." A stanza is a batch of lines arranged in some definite order of line-length and rhyme-scheme.

Prose and Verse are antithetical terms : Prose and Poetry are not.

Poetry depends for its existence not on its form but on its content. It is more usually expressed in verse as being a fitter instrument, but much lofty prose is, in its nature, poetry.

Conversely, much that is written in verse is not poetry.

A good illustration may be found in Bunyan's *Pilgrim's Progress*. The introduction is written in verse and is anything but poetry, while the great prose work of the allegory itself often rises to fine poetic heights.

Before attempting to scan a passage or even a single line the whole poem should be considered, or at least the essential context, in order to determine the basic pattern —the pattern referred to in the definition. However obscure the metrical pattern there generally occurs a line here and there which yields up the secret, and this we may call the " betraying " line. At the same time, a single line may be very misleading, and should never be

set in an examination paper unless some clue is given as
to the basic pattern, or unless the examiner is prepared
to accept any reasonable scansion of the line itself, re-
gardless of the context. Here is a line in point :—

" How many sailors in how many ships ? "

I venture to assert that if the pattern of the whole poem
is not known most people would scan the line thus :—

" Hów many | saílors in | hów many | shíps ? "

on a four-foot dactylic base with catalectic last foot.

But the whole poem is written on a five-foot iambic
base, and therefore the true scansion should be :—

" How má | ny saí | lors in | how má | ny shíps ? "

And this gives rise to another point.

An important rule in scansion is to mark the *natural*
speech stresses before attempting to divide into feet. But
sometimes the question arises as to which is the natural
stress. In the two ways of scanning the above line it
will be seen that some of the stresses are different. And
so we get this subsidiary rule :—that it is permissible
slightly to enforce or slightly to weaken a natural stress
in order to bring it into conformity with the basic pattern,
provided that the accent is not thereby wrenched so as to
destroy the accepted pronunciation.

Yet another point which arises out of this difference in
scansion is to show the value of a knowledge of prosody.
A natural ear for rhythm is, of course, far more valuable
than a scientific understanding of prosody, but even a
good natural ear for rhythm will be all the better for that
extra bit of prosodic knowledge.

Look at this :—

" And will any say when my bell of quittance is heard
        in the gloom,
    And a crossing breeze cuts a pause in its outrollings,
Till they rise again, as they were a new bell's boom,
    ' He hears it not now, but used to notice such
        things ' ? "

Afterwards. THOMAS HARDY.

We find from the whole poem, and exemplified in this
stanza, that the pattern is one of alternate six-foot and
five-foot lines.   So that the third line should run :—

" Till they ríse | agáin, | as they wére | a néw | béll's |
    bóom."
Not like this, as I have so often heard it spoken :—
" Till they ríse | agáin, | as they wére | a néw | bell's
    bóom."

The correct scansion, giving the line its due six feet belonging to the pattern, stresses the boom and hammer-
stroke of the bell.

Now let us tabulate a few simple rules for scanning :—

1.   Read the poem carefully, or at least read enough
of the context to determine the basic pattern.   Look for
the " betraying " line.

2.   Mark the natural speech stresses.

3.   Divide into feet with reference to the basic pattern,
so that every foot in the basic pattern is represented in
the spoken line, though not necessarily identical with it.

Let us take a simple example :—

" God who created me
      Nimble and light of limb,
In three elements free,
      To run, to ride, to swim :
Not when the sense is dim,
      But now from the heart of joy,
I would remember Him ;
      Take the thanks of a boy."

Prayers. H. C. BEECHING.

The first line can be misleading, and if we do not look
at the rest of the stanza we shall most likely scan it as a
line of two dactyls :—

Gód who cre | áted me.

But there is a betraying line,

      To run, to ride, to swim.

This can only be scanned in one way, and it gives us the
basic pattern of three iambic feet.

$$- \acute{} \mid - \acute{} \mid - \acute{}$$

Now let us scan the poem all through with reference to
this base.

" Gód | who creá | ted me
      Nímble | and líght | of límb,
In thrée | élements | frée,
      To rún, | to ríde, | to swím :
Nót when | the sénse | is dím,
      But nów | from the héart | of jóy,
Í would | remém | ber Hím ;
      ∧ Táke | the thánks | of a bóy."

In the first line I would regard " God " as a monosyllabic foot by reason of its importance. In the last line, however, the word " take " has a lesser value, and so should be regarded not as a monosyllabic foot, but as one that lacks the opening weak stress—an acephalous foot, or a line with initial truncation.

Another point :

It would be possible, without altering the natural stresses or destroying the pattern, to scan the first line thus :—

Gód who | creá | ted me.

One cannot say that this is *wrong,* but it seems to me to weaken the word " God," and so to take away from the value of the first line. From this we may deduce that there may be more than one possible scansion of a line, none of which can be condemned as actually *wrong,* although it may be felt that one way is better than another. That is not to say that any scansion can be accepted as a possible variation; there is such a thing as a wrong scansion.

Let us take the opening line of *Paradise Lost :—*

" Of Mán's | fírst | disobé | dience, | and the frúit." [1]

A possible scansion, I suppose, would be :—

Of Mán's | fírst dis | obé | dience, | and the frúit.

Now look at this :—

Of Mán's | first dís | obé | dience, | and the frúit.

If the line were scanned in this way there would be an entirely unnecessary displacement of the natural speech stress, and so far it must be regarded as a wrong scansion.

[1] This, I maintain, is the most satisfactory scansion.

But a more definitely wrong scansion would be this :—

Of Mán's | fírst diso | bédience, | and the frúit.

Here the fundamental rule that every foot in the basic pattern must be represented in the spoken line is disregarded. The basic pattern is the normal blank verse line of five iambic feet. That is not a possible variation, but a definitely wrong scansion.

There may be disagreement about the basic pattern which cannot be dispelled by any betraying line. Here is a case in point, *The Death of Admiral Blake*, by Newbolt.

I had a fierce argument with a colleague as to the correct scansion of this poem. He maintained that the whole poem should be treated as rising rhythm—anapæsts and iambs : I affirmed that the poet intended the longer lines to be a falling rhythm—dactyls and trochees —and the shorter lines to be a deliberate contrast of rising rhythm. The poet was dead : there could be no appeal there. So I wrote to Prof. Saintsbury and put the question to him. His judgment was that of Solomon. He said that he himself preferred the rising rhythm for the whole poem, but he felt that the poet intended the contrast of falling and rising rhythm.

Here is the first stanza :—

" Laden with spoil of the South, fulfilled with the glory
      of achievement,
   And freshly crowned with never dying fame,
Sweeping by shores where the names are the names of
      the victories of England,
   Across the Bay the squadron homeward came."

Just a word about notation. It is not advisable to use the classical signs long — and short ᴗ. These are quantitative signs, the principal element in classical verse being quantity. In modern verse, although quantity has a definite place, the principal element is stress, and very often a strong stress will coincide with a short quantity, and vice versa. It is rather distressing to any one with a sense of quantitative values to see the word "shadow," for instance, notated as "shādŏw." It should be "shádow," or more fully "shádōw."

For much the same reason it is, I think, advisable to avoid using the terms Dimeter, Trimeter, Tetrameter, Pentameter, Hexameter, etc. The Greeks applied these terms according to the nature of the feet composing the line. A "meter" was a metrical unit which was capable of exact division. Now the iamb consisted of a short and a long syllable, the long being twice the length of the short; therefore the iamb was not capable of exact division, and was therefore not a meter. Consequently, the Greek dramatic line used by Æschylus, Sophocles and Euripides, which was basically six iambic feet with resolutions into trochees, anapæsts, pyrrhics and spondees, was not a hexameter but a trimeter, consisting of three meters, or three *pairs* of iambs.

Contrariwise, the six-foot line employed by Homer, which consisted of mixed dactyls and spondees, was a hexameter, because each foot was capable of exact division and was therefore a meter. So do not speak of the normal Blank Verse or Heroic line as Iambic Pentameter, but as a line of five iambic feet. An iambic pentameter line would have to consist of ten feet, or five pairs of iambs. In the same way the line of *Hiawatha* is correctly " trochaic dimeter " ; while Tennyson's *Locksley Hall* is " trochaic tetrameter catalectic."

Let me take another point :

Shelley's *Skylark* is undoubtedly written in falling rhythm for the first four lines of each stanza, while the last line is in striking contrast with the rest of the pattern, being twice the length and in rising rhythm—an Alexandrine (not a Hexameter).

Then how does one explain this stanza?

> " What objects are the fountains
>> Of thy happy strain?
> What lakes or fields or mountains?
>> What shapes of sky or plain?
> What love of thine own kind?   What ignorance of
>> pain? "

Are we to explain this as a stanza suddenly shoved into the pattern entirely in rising rhythm? No, the first, third and fourth lines are examples of anacrusis, that is, beginning with a weak-stressed syllable which is really outside the metrical pattern; so that the scansion should be :—

> " What) óbjects | are the | foúntains
>> Of thy | háppy | stráin?
> What) lákes or | fiélds or | móuntains?
>> What) shápes of | ský or | pláin?
> What lóve | of thíne | own kínd? | What íg | norance |
>> of páin? "

Now let us suppose that for some cranky reason we take this stanza as the norm, and attempt to scan the rest of the poem in conformity with it. Let us take the opening stanza :—

> " Hail to thee, blithe spirit,
> Bird thou never wert ;
> That from Heav'n or near it
> Pourest thy full heart
> In profuse strains of unpremeditated art."

To scan this throughout in rising rhythm we shall have to do this :—

> " Háil | to thée, | blithe spír(it
> Bírd | thou né | ver wért ;
> ∧ Thát | from Héav'n | or néar it
> ∧ Póur | est thý | fúll héart
> In pró | fuse stráins | of ún | preméd | itá | ted árt."

The words " hail " and " bird " which now form the first foot of lines one and two may possibly be considered as monosyllabic feet, in which the words are regarded as filling out the whole foot ; but this cannot be the case with lines three and four. In these latter cases, as also probably in the two former, the feet must be regarded as " acephalous," literally " without a head," or as cases of initial truncation.

From this we can deduce the following :—

An iambic line scanned trochaically becomes anacrustic ; a trochaic line scanned iambically becomes acephalous.

The correct scansion of this stanza should be :—

" Háil to | thée, blithe | spírit!
Bírd thou | néver | wért;
Thát from | Héav'n or | néar it
Póurest | thý fúll | héart
In pró | fuse stráins | of ún | premé | ditá | ted árt."

Here are a few suggested scansions of more difficult
poems.

Í have | hád | pláymates | ⌒ | Í have | hád com |
pánions | ⌒

In my | dáys of | chíldhood | ⌒ | in my | jóyful | schóol-
days | ⌒

Áll, | áll are | gone | ⋀ the | óld fa | míliar | fáces | ⌒

     *   *   *   *

I | háve a | fríend | ⋀ a | kínder | fríend has | nó man | ⌒

Líke | ⋀ an | íngrate | ⋀ I | léft my | fríend a | brúptly | ⌒

Léft him | ⋀ to | múse | on the | óld fa | míliar |
fáces | ⌒ [1]

It is suggested that this poem consists basically of eight
trochaic feet, the last foot in each line being expressed
by a metrical pause. There are frequent metrical pauses,
sometimes extending over a whole foot, sometimes only
covering the strong stress of the trochee.   In line 2 of the
second stanza quoted one gets the effect of a tied note in
music.

It would no doubt be possible to scan this poem by the
use of pæons, but that is an unnecessary use of an unusual foot, and it is better to avoid using unusual foot-

[1] *The Old Familiar Faces,* Charles Lamb.

measures. Even the amphibrach is better avoided and can nearly always be dispensed with. As a basic foot it gives an ugly and almost sea-sick movement, and can nearly always be avoided by a quite legitimate re-barring into either dactyls or anapæsts, more usually the latter.

Shý | as the | squírrel | ∧ and | wáyward | as the | swállow, | ⌢

    Swíft | as the | swállow | ∧ a | lóng the | rívers | líght | ⌢

Círcle | ting the | súrface | ∧ to | méet his | mírror'd | wínglets | ⌢

       ♩♩

    Fléeter | ∧ she | séems | in her | stáy than | in her | flíght. | ⌢

Shý | as the | squírrel | ∧ that | léaps a | mong the | píne-tops | ⌢

    Wáyward | as the | swállow | over | héad at | sét of | sún, | ⌢

Shé | whom I | lóve | ∧ is | hárd to | cátch and | cónquer, | ⌢

    Hárd, but | Ó the | glóry | of the | wínning | were she | wón ! | ⌢ [1]

This is again basically a line of eight trochaic feet. Lines 6 and 8 are " betraying " lines.

Line 4 shows another example of the musical tied note effect.

Trámping | at níght | in the cóld | and wét | I pássed | the lígh | ted ínn | ⌢

And an óld | túne, | a swéet | túne, | was bé | ing pláyed | withín | ⌢

    [1] *Love in the Valley,* George Meredith.

It was fúll | of the láugh | of the léaves | ⌒ | and the
    sóng | the wínd | síngs; | ⌒
It bróught | the téars | and the chóked | thróat, | and a
    cátch | to the héart | -stríngs | ⌒ [2]

Here we have an 8 foot line of rising rhythm, in mixed
iambs and anapæsts, with occasional substitution of
monosyllabic feet, and one trochaic inversion at the beginning of line 1. The last foot of each line is a metrical
pause, and there is also a metrical pause at the 4th foot
of line 3.

The musical tied note effect is found here at the monosyllabic feet where the value of the previous word laps
over into the monosyllabic foot.

Phrasing

PHRASING is the grouping of words in the way which is
best calculated to bring out the meaning.

A phrase is a group of words making sense. Phrases
may vary in length almost infinitely from a single word
to a passage of several lines.

" Halt!   Who goes there? "
There are two phrases here, the first consisting of the
single word " Halt."

Here is an example of an unusually long phrase from
Galsworthy's poem *Errantry.*

---

[2] *Personal,* Masefield.

> " Ah! for the summons of a challenge cry
> Which sets to swinging fast the bell that tolls
> The high and leaping chimes of sympathy
> Within that true cathedral of our souls
> Set in our bodies' jeering market-place . . . "

Here a breath may well be taken after the first line, although there is no punctuation mark; it is an ejaculatory phrase which stands easily alone. But from lines 2 to 5 inclusive there is no entirely satisfactory break, and it would be better, if it can be done without strain, to speak these four lines on one breath. If this is not practicable, a quick renewal of breath had better be made after " sympathy."

A phrase being a " sense-group " it follows that all the words forming the phrase belong very closely together, and nothing should be done in speaking the phrase to spoil or break this " belongingness." Therefore it is desirable that a phrase should be spoken on one breath. In the case of long phrases this means that a good delivery of the phrase largely depends on good breath control.

In some extreme cases it is impossible to obey this rule, and some point must be chosen where the breath may be taken without any perceptible join.

It is often better deliberately to break a long phrase than to speak it on one breath and cause a sense of strain either to the speaker or to his hearers. It is possible silently to renew a breath, if it is not a very deep one, without any one being aware of it, if the directions given on pages 20 and 21 for silent inhalation are followed.

A good test for phrasing and breath-control is afforded by Turner's poem *Ecstasy*. In the second stanza, for instance, the second, third and fourth lines should be spoken on one breath:—

" The wind had graven their small eager hands
To feel the forests and the dark nights of Asia
Behind the purple bloom of the horizon —"

The whole of the last stanza, although it is actually composed of many phrases, would be ideally spoken on one breath, or at least down to the word " sang " in the last line. This would preserve the limpid quality of the diction, and the " ecstatic " effect of the cumulative wind, stars, clouds and sky, reaching the climax in " I sang," with a circumflex falling inflection on " sang."

Sarah Bernhardt said that one should be able to speak four lines in one breath. She was speaking of French Alexandrines, lines of six iambic feet, making a total of twenty-four feet, and she instances four lines of *Phèdre* which she used to deliver in one breath.

The last stanza of *Ecstasy* down to " sang " contains only twenty-one feet, so this should not be impossible.

Interpretation and Characterization

ALL prose and verse selections must be interpreted but only dramatic work can be characterized as well.

And here arises the whole question of personality.

Let us think, then, of dramatic work first.

One sometimes reads of an actor entirely submerging

his own personality, and this is supposed to be high. praise. To begin with, I maintain that this is impossible. If a player seems to sink his own personality to that extent, it means that he never possessed very much. The greater the artist the greater the personality, and the ideal at which to aim in performance is to combine one's own personality with that of the character one is portraying.

I once won two guineas in a competition which offered the prize for a definition of " impersonation " in not more than ten words. I wrote:—" The blending of two personalities, the actor and the acted," and I still think I earned that two guineas.

That is part of the interest in seeing various Hamlets. If every Hamlet submerged his personality—if that were possible, which it isn't—the result would be deadly boredom. So do not be afraid of the great gift of personality. At the same time do not exploit it to the submerging of the personality you are portraying—which *is* possible.

Another point in regard to characterization is that a generous latitude should be allowed to students to express their own ideas. Any originality of thought should be encouraged so long as it is not at variance with the facts. A meek and mild Lady Macbeth, a managing Cordelia, a cold-blooded Othello or a temperate Cassius would be unthinkable.

It is often maintained that, in the speaking of poems, everything should be done to sink one's own personality, so that the poet's words come to the listener's ears without any obstructing middle element. To this end inflection is practically eliminated and the delivery approximated to a monotone. The same idea lies behind the practice of intoning the Gospel in the Mass, that no human personality should obtrude itself between the Word of God and the congregation. However that may be as regards the ritual of the Mass, to apply it to the speaking of poems is, surely, to lose all sense of proportion. An expressionless robot is all that is necessary. This idea was carried to its logical conclusion on an occasion when a reciter gave a concert in a London hall, and spoke the poems from behind a curtain, so that the recitalist was never seen at all. Whether this admirable modesty was carried to the length of withholding the speaker's name, I do not know. In such cases it is indeed *Vox et praeterea nihil.*

I remember hearing a dual speaking of *The Lady of Shalott* by two excellent and well-known elocutionists who employed a clear monotone varied by an occasional musical interval, usually a minor third. The effect for a time was curiously soothing, but presently I found myself slipping into a state of semiconsciousness, lulled and drugged by this monotonous chant. Why, oh! why do really talented reciters waste their gifts so? Let us hold a balance, and remember the beautiful word " proportion," and avoid the extremes of over-indulgence in personal expression on the one side, and a deadly utterance of mere words without colour or inflection, indeed devoid of all technical or emotional variation, on the other.

Remember, too, that the voice is not the only mode of

expression; there remain the face, gesture and bodily movement. Dramatic work affords plenty of scope for the use of these things. Let us think of gesture and general poise.

Without dealing scientifically and exhaustively with the subject, as, for instance, in the case of the Delsarte system, here are a few general principles which will, I think, be found helpful. First, look to the stance and general poise of the body. This has been treated in the chapter on breathing. No gesture or movement will be expressive unless the body is elastic and well poised. starting from this basic condition think next of the arms, hands and fingers. There must be no constriction of any of the limbs. If there is any lack of freedom in the fingers, for instance, try this exercise:—Take hold of the hand just below the wrist, letting the hand drop limply; then shake the hand up and down, not by its own volition but by the action of the forearm. This ensures the quiescence of the antagonistic muscles, and the active muscles are now in a right condition for making a free and expressive gesture. The fingers must never be bunched but freely separated, the forefinger leading and the others, as it were, backing it up.

To free the arms, stand bent slightly forwards with the arms hanging freely from the shoulders. Then swing the arms from right to left, *not by their own volition,* but by the swinging action of the body.

Now, standing erect, raise the arm, employing the muscles in the *upper* arm, the forearm rising only, as it were, because it is attached to the upper arm. Only when the arm is at shoulder level send the vital message along the forearm and the hand to the very tips of the fingers.

Nearly all arm gestures should arise, physically, from the shoulder. One should not be conscious of the elbow unless it is a matter of Old Comedy, when the period clothes with the lace ruffles of the men and the habit of taking snuff, and the panniers of the ladies give a special significance to the elbow.

Remember, too, that gesture is a form of emphasis, and should not be employed unless it is felt that it will add something to the interpretation.

It is a generally accepted rule that gesture should not be used in speaking non-dramatic verse, and as a guiding principle this is good. But do not let us be hidebound in this matter. There may arise occasions when the artistic perception may prompt one to make some action, and—personally—I would not rule it out. There is, for instance, the kind of poem which Browning labels " dramatic lyrics," in which the story is dramatic while the verse-form and diction are lyrical. Be guided by your good sense and feeling of artistic " justness."

In conclusion, a word of warning.

Important though it is to have a proper understanding of the technical means and modes of expression, it must never be forgotten that technique alone is dead, and that you will never become a complete artist until the necessary mechanism is so oiled and smoothly running that its presence is never obtruded. Technique is the necessary vehicle by means of which the soul and spirit can express themselves through the body.

I am reminded of a sermon in which the preacher startled his congregation by declaring that if he were asked whether he possessed a soul he would answer " No ! "   After leaving his hearers shocked and scandalized for a moment he proceeded :   " Man has no soul : Man *has* a body : Man *is* a soul."   That is to say, the essential part of man is not his body but that which inhabits his body.   And so we must make this framework as pliant as possible for the expression of the real man inside.   Remember *that* in regard to technique, and don't make the mistake of thinking that, if only one understands and feels aright, the expression will be equally satisfactory.   It *won't!*   This is a point which needs stressing. It is generally those who have a certain natural facility of expression who are impatient of technique. But do not let yourself be deceived.   However talented you may be, even to the point of genius, your gifts will largely be wasted unless you are content to begin at the beginning and learn your A B C.

In his later plays the changing position of the cæsura was one of the many ways by which Shakspere varied his Blank Verse. (See page 49.)

> " This supernatural soliciting
> Cannot be ill; cannot be good: if ill,
> Why hath it given me earnest of success,
> Commencing in a truth? I am Thane of Cawdor:
> If good, why do I yield to that suggestion
> Whose horrid image doth unfix my hair
> And make my seated heart knock at my ribs,
> Against the use of nature? Present fears
> Are less than horrible imaginings:
> My thought, whose murder yet is but fantastical,
> Shakes so my single state of man that function
> Is smothered in surmise, and nothing is
> But what is not.

Line 1. No cæsura.

„ 2. Cæsura at end of fourth foot. If there is more than one pause in a line the cæsura is the most important.

„ 3. No cæsura.

„ 4. Cæsura at end of third foot.

„ 5. Cæsura at end of first foot.

„ 6. Cæsura at half of third foot.

„ 7. Cæsura at end of third foot.

„ 8. Cæsura at half of fourth foot.

„ 9. No cæsura.

„ 10. Cæsura at end of first foot.

„ 11. Cæsura at end of fourth foot.

„ 12. Cæsura at end of third foot.